STEPPING UP

*Wholeness Ethics for Prisoners
and Those Who Care About Them*

by Troy K. Chapman

For Maryann,
a whole-souled mother of goodness
and my partner in both love and labor.
You increase my wholeness.

TABLE OF CONTENTS

Introduction

❖ *You like drinking coffee but don't have money to buy any. Your cell mate keeps a jar in his locker and never locks it. He likely wouldn't notice a few spoons of missing coffee and even if he did he wouldn't be able to prove it. Is it wrong to help yourself to some of his coffee?*

❖ *You're on the yard with a group of men whose opinions and friendship mean a lot to you. An old man slips on the ice nearby and your first impulse is to make sure he's all right and help him up. Before you can act, however, one of your friends who knows about the old man's case says, "It serves you right, child molester." Everyone laughs and more insults are spoken. Do you follow or suppress your instinct to help another human being in distress? And if you do act, what do you say to your friends?*

❖ *Or, as happened to a man in Detroit recently, you find out your son has sexually abused your daughter. This man killed his son. How would you respond?*

Life is a never-ending series of these dilemmas in which we're called to decide what is the right thing to do. Just as important as *what* to do, however, is *why* we do it.

Why do we decide to act one way instead of another? What principles (or absence of principles, for that matter) govern our thinking, our actions and our lives? Who chooses these principles, us or someone else? And what were the criteria for choosing them?

Or maybe you live by the old saying, "If it feels good, do it." This may feel like freedom but as the philosopher Immanuel Kant pointed out, we don't choose our desires, impulses, and appetites, so to allow them to govern us is a form of enslavement, not freedom. We're no more free when we follow them than a worm is when it follows its impulse to dig into an apple.

It used to make me feel good to impress my friends. I spent a lot of time and energy thinking of ways to do so. I never questioned their values or their intentions. I just blindly did what I thought would make them like me. This is a normal stage of adolescence but sometimes it becomes a habit we carry into adulthood. This is especially true if we don't consciously choose what principles will guide our lives. When we don't have our own center we tend to revolve around things outside ourselves.

This was true of me and it led me through

alcoholism, drug abuse, broken relationships and prison before I turned 21 years old. It culminated when I killed a man in a bar fight in 1984 and was sentenced to 60-90 years.

When I came back to prison I had to face the truth that the way I had been living was completely bankrupt. Behind me was misery, shame and failure. I had taken a young man's life and had senselessly devastated his family as well as mine. In front of me was 60 years of prison which, from what I could see at the time, amounted to 60 years of mindlessly trying to escape the reality of my life and avoid facing myself. This is what prison represented to me. Still, somewhere in me was a glimmer of hope that something could be salvaged from this bleak rubble. I had no hope for happiness or anything like it but thought that perhaps I might atone in some small way for my past and find some meaning in that. I've since learned that meaning is the foundation of all true happiness anyway. I've also learned that meaning is connected to the question of which principles guide our lives.

But I didn't know any of this then. At that time I was just groping in the dark. I had no idea what was good or how I might go about moving toward it. What I had were questions. I wanted to know what was worthy of spending my time (and life) pursuing. What principles should guide me? What matters and what doesn't? Which values are more important than others?

There were many more questions but they all boiled down to one: What is the good life and how does one achieve and live it? I had very little education but thanks to a third grade teacher named Marguerite Feller — who would become a pivotal person in my life — I knew how to read. I began reading philosophy, ethics, classical literature, spirituality and anything else I thought might speak to my question.

The first part of this question — what is the good life? — was key to answering the second part of how to achieve it. Was the good life having a lot of stuff? Experiencing a lot of pleasure? Winning? If so, then the good life was likely out of my reach. I was probably never going to have a lot of stuff and most of the pleasures people chase in prison didn't lead to the good life as far as I could see. As to winning, just being here made me a loser by any social standard I might have cared about.

I kept digging. Trying to get a general sense, I asked if the good life was about "getting" at all. We think this way at first: The good life is about me being happy. Plato called this "the prized life" — a life of comfort, wealth and privilege, maybe like a movie star or rapper. It's prized by both the person living it and onlookers.

But then I thought maybe the good life isn't about how life treats me. Maybe it's about how I treat life. Said differently, maybe it's more about what I give than what I get. Lives focused more on giving than getting were call "praised" by Plato. While people didn't necessarily want to live those lives, they could praise them as good. The lives of Abraham Lincoln or Martin Luther King, Jr., might be examples of this. Was this the good life? I wasn't sure, so I continued on with my question.

This question stretches back to the beginnings of philosophy. In my readings I came across the Greek word "eudaimonia." This has been translated into English as "happiness" but some have criticized this translation, pointing out that what Aristotle meant when he called this the "ultimate good" was something more than the word happiness means in our time. Eudaimonia means something closer to "well-being" and "human flourishing." It refers more to overall soundness or wellness — which includes what we think of as happiness but isn't limited to that.

For me the concept seemed closer to wholeness, and this became my answer to the first half of my question: The good life is the life that creates wholeness. I eventually came to define wholeness as peace, balance and beneficence (more about that in Chapter 1). As to the question of whether getting or giving was better, it seemed to me that the concept of wholeness dissolved that question. It was a false choice. The good life must create wholeness in myself *and* in the world.

As to the second half of the question — the "how" — the path to wholeness is a direct one: We create wholeness by putting wholeness at the center of our thinking and using it as the measure of right and wrong, good and bad.

This is something that seemed possible even here in prison. I couldn't quite conceive of "becoming whole" but I knew I could at least begin trying to do what increased wholeness.

I set myself to that task and over time I began to think of this way of living as "wholeness ethics." It brings together many threads from many directions; you might hear in it echoes of Aristotle, Jesus and St. Paul, Thomas Aquinas, Albert Schweitzer, and Albert Einstein. You may recognize the influences of Mohandas Gandhi, Martin Luther King, Jr., Fyodor Dostoyevsky, Nelson Mandela, Viktor Frankl, Black Elk and Chief Seattle, Ralph Waldo Emerson and my beloved poets Rumi and Rainer Maria Rilke. So wholeness ethics was born, not from any one tradition, but from many.

Later, as I began discussing it informally with men here who were conducting their own version of the search described above, we came together and with the help of supportive staff, started meeting weekly as the Kinross Ethics Project and building community around this way of living. Iron sharpens iron and my understanding of wholeness ethics developed even further in discussions with these dedicated, sincere and intelligent men.

This book is an extension of all this.

Structurally, it is based on the eight-week syllabus of the Ethics Project. We have two- to four-hour discussions on each of these sections; so if you're not in a prison where there's a group I would encourage you to read the book with at least one other person and talk about it as you do so. There are suggested exercises at the end of each chapter. If these help, use them; if they don't, make up your own. The important thing to remember is that this book, like ethics itself, in my view, is about relationship. It's about being in relationship in ways that make us all more whole. Thus, to read it in any form of community (again, even with one other person) is to encounter it on a richer level. There's no magic formula here, but our relationships transform us for good or ill throughout our lives. Wholeness ethics is a way of living that guides this transformation toward greater wholeness.

My own life bears witness to the fact that prison is no barrier to this process. In fact it may, like a monastery, facilitate it. Which means that we can use our time here for this purpose — to become whole and turn ourselves into agents of wholeness — or we can continue the very thinking and behavior that brought us here. That seems to me nothing if not a form of self hatred. But the choice is yours. And since you've picked up this book, maybe you've already reached the conclusion that it's time to try something different. If so we'll be traveling together.

A Word to Non-Prisoners

In Chapter 7 of this book I discuss something called "the myth of non-connection." It's the belief that certain things are not connected to, and have no bearing on, one's life. One version of this myth led us, not so long ago, to believe that various parts of the ecosystem were not connected to other parts. We've since learned that that thinking was wrong. If we dump toxic waste in a river "over there," it has a way of finding its way back to us "over here."

Yet in present-day America, the myth of non-connection is alive and well in other forms. For example, many Americans who have no personal connection with prisoners or prisons believe that this institution has no bearing on their lives. Like other forms of pollution in earlier times, the belief holds that if we dump this human pollution "over there" it becomes irrelevant to us "over here."

This of course is no more true of people than it is of chemicals. Prisoners and free Americans are two plants growing up out of the same ground. We share not only a physical ecosystem but a non-physical one as well. If a superbug develops here in prison, for instance, it won't be long before free people are dying from it. The same is true if vicious strains of ignorance and hatred develop here. This is the first premise of wholeness ethics: we're in this together — whether we like it or not.

If you don't know anyone in prison you might have looked at the title of this book and thought, "This has nothing to do with me." If so, remember that the myth of non-connection is indeed a myth. It's true that "Stepping Up" is written to prisoners, but the philosophy of wholeness ethics is universal; there's something here for anyone interested in living more soundly — whether in prison or not.

Besides, with the media's obsession with showing only the sensational and negative aspects of prison (part of the comic-book consciousness that dominates our culture) here's something a little more nuanced and positive about and from prison. If for no other reason, it's worth reading to balance the stereotype.

Lastly, if nothing else, this book, like the distance between us as human beings, has the virtue of being short. Think of it as a short trip to prison for a minor crime. Well, maybe not. How about: if you've read this far, don't be a quitter. Read on.

CHAPTER 1
What Is Ethics?
(And Why Should You Care?)

We don't see things as they are,
we see things as we are. —*Anaïs Nin*

YOUR MAP OF REALITY

Take a minute and bring to mind a place you know well, a part of your neighborhood out in the world or the route you travel from your unit to work every day, for instance. Any place you're familiar with will do.

The moment you called this place to mind, what happened? A map popped into your head, right? I'm not necessarily talking about a visual map. Perhaps yours is visual, or maybe it's just a memory impression, but it's still a map.

This is what our brains do with places we've been. They create mental maps of these places. Not only that, but if someone begins describing an area near an area you're familiar with, your brain will begin adding what this person tells you to the map it has already made. Even if you've never been to the place, you'll begin to "see" it in your mind.

Now, if your own observations and those of others are accurate, you'll be able to travel through these areas simply by looking at your mental maps. In fact, we do this so often in so many different ways that we almost don't notice it unless we stop to think about it. But the fact is, our heads are chock full of maps.

The reason we're interested in this is that we don't just make maps of places. We make maps of everything. If you've ever baked a cake, put oil in your car, tied your shoes, or changed your underwear (and I hope you've done at least one of these) you have a map of the process in your brain. If you can whistle or hum a tune it's because you've heard the tune, made a map of it, and are following that map as you play back the melody. In fact, everything you've ever done in your life, everything anyone else has ever told you about — even if you thought they were lying or crazy and you made a mental guess at the truth — has been turned into a map in your brain. In addition to this you have a mental map of all the places you've *never* been and all the things you've *never* experienced.

How can that be?

If you've ever seen really old maps from ancient times, you may remember seeing dragons and sea monsters around the edges.

These were areas that the mapmaker didn't know; they were uncharted. Perhaps ships had sailed into these areas and hadn't come back, or they came back with tales of strange things that people didn't understand. All of this was represented by dragons or sea monsters. So, even though people didn't know exactly what was in these places, they were still represented on maps.

The same is true of us. When we don't know something we simply draw in what we imagine might be there. All of us remember doing this when we were young around the topic of sex — especially with our knowledge of the opposite sex. Ask any boy of a certain age what he knows about girls (which is asking him to show you his map about girls) and you're apt to get some interesting looking dragons. Or ask any person what lies beyond death or beyond the furthest reaches of space and the same is true.

So we make maps of everything — of places, of ideas, of philosophies, of groups of people, of relationships. If we put together all the maps we've made of individual things we end up with one big map that might be called our map of reality. This is our mental picture of the world, truth, ourselves, others and every other thing we've ever encountered in the world or even in our minds.

What shape is your map of reality in?

We then refer to this map as we travel through life. Our map of reality tells us what to expect and how to act (which road to take) in various situations. If I come upon a barking dog and my map tells me "Dogs are mean and unpredictable," I'm going to act one way; if my map tells me "Dogs love me," I'm going to act another way.

All good so far. We make maps and we use them to get around in life. But what happens if a map is wrong? Imagine you want to go from Point A to Point B. You pick up a map or create one yourself but it's completely messed up. It's got roads mislabeled, roads indicated where there are none, swamps and rivers where the actual roads are, and so on. How well are you going to travel using this map?

And what if Point B, the place we want to get to, isn't a physical place? What if we're reading screwed-up maps to places like "Success," "Happiness," "Manhood," "Honor" and "The Good Life"?

This has happened to many of us because our ideas of how to get to these places are inaccurate. We've turned these inaccuracies into maps and ended up in the middle of various sinkholes.

Many people who were given a map that said "Follow the money road to reach happiness" have spent years on that road and never reached happiness. Many young boys were given maps that said "Violence is the way to manhood." We followed these maps and found ourselves in the ditch of ruined relationships with everyone, including ourselves.

When I came to prison and started looking at the maps I had been using, I found that many of them were screwed up. Prison was not on the list of places I wanted to go in life. I came here because I had a bad map that promised to take me somewhere good. If I had had an accurate map with an arrow saying "Prison This Way," I would have taken a different turn. When I realized this I began pulling out my many different maps and checking, correcting and redrawing them.

I've thought a lot about where I wanted to go in life (and where I still want to go for that matter). What was I searching for when I was chasing money, sex, drugs, pleasure and so on? I think, behind all other things, what I wanted more than anything else was just to be whole. This was the reason I was trying to reconfigure all my maps of reality — so I could follow them to wholeness.

If I have a map of women, for example, do I want one that leads merely to sex? This is one of the things men are told in our culture: all we really need to know about women is how to get them in bed. That might sound good until we've done it for a few years and we tire of the manipulative mind behind it, and of the emptiness of not having deeper connections. So we say "I want a map of women that leads to wholeness." The same with "Work," "Citizenship," "Manhood," "Womanhood," "Honor," "Prosperity," etc.

WHOLENESS ETHICS

As the name implies, wholeness ethics is about living in ways that increase wholeness in ourselves and in the world. Another name for wholeness ethics is wholism. Wholists practice wholeness ethics and advocate them in our world. Thus we will talk about ways of thinking and behaving that are "wholistic" or "un-wholistic" (also known a bit more colorfully as "a-holistic").

The maxim of wholeness ethics is:

Do only what increases wholeness in yourself and in the world.

Wholeness is defined as peace, balance and beneficence. Peace refers to the energy of well-being and enoughness. This energy can be generated by our circumstances — as when we're surrounded by people who love us — but we must also learn to generate it within ourselves when circumstances outside us are not so favorable. Balance is a state of right relationship between opposing, contrasting or interacting elements. It's about keeping things in proportion and being aware of when we're giving things too much or not enough energy and attention. Beneficence is beneficial energy, thought or action. It is creative and active goodness.

Another word for wholeness is *integrity*, which means "completeness, unity and soundness." *Wholeness* is related to the word *integrate*, which means "to make into a whole" and so is also related to *disintegrate*, which means to separate into pieces or to fragment.

Why should you care about wholeness ethics? Imagine you've been dropped into the wilderness like one of those survival guys we see on TV. A week later, you've been chased by a badger, eaten alive by insects, and you've poisoned yourself several times trying to figure out what plants are edible. Then one day, while crawling out from behind the tree where you've been vomiting after eating some bad mushrooms, you find a book there on the ground. It's entitled "The Happy Camper's Guide to Thriving in the Wilderness." Why should you care about the information contained in that guide?

The answer is that the information in that guide will increase the quality of your life. If you learn how to avoid badgers, keep the insects away and identify the various plants and mushrooms that are edible, your life is suddenly improved in major ways. The same is true in the "wilderness of life." When we learn what increases peace, balance and beneficence — in other words, what is wholistic — our lives are also improved in major ways.

Our hypothetical "Happy Camper's Guide" is a map to living a good life in the wilderness. The book you hold in your hands is a map to the good life.

If you want to live a more meaningful and healthy life and inhabit a saner, more wholesome world, then you should care about wholeness ethics. In the coming chapters, we're going to talk about the principles, challenges and rewards of living wholistically. If you choose to adopt this way of thinking into your life, you will be like the person who finds the wilderness guide, reads it and applies it to his daily life from that point forward. When he comes upon a mushroom, he will check the guide to see if it's edible or not. When he's ready to camp for the night he'll apply the principles contained in the guide. Over time he'll create a more and more accurate mental map for living well in the wilderness.

This is one way of approaching this book or course. Another approach is to coast through this information without really putting forth any effort and still expect your life to magically change. This is like a person hurriedly reading the wilderness guide, then tossing it back into the bushes before trekking back into the wild, thinking "I've got this now." We can pretty much predict the result of this attitude. Such a person, if he or she survives at all, will likely suffer countless unnecessary hardships.

Wholeness ethics isn't magical information that will change your life. If you get up every morning and choose to live wholistically, your life will be transformed, but it will be the daily living in right relationship that transforms things, not the information — just as it's traveling that gets you from one place to another and not the map-reading.

IF YOU WANT TO BE AN ETHICAL EINSTEIN (SOMEDAY)... *Fold a piece of paper in half once, then again. This will give you four sections on each side for a total of eight. Number them from 1 to 8. As you read each of the eight chapters in this book or finish each of the eight classroom sessions, write down in each section at least two things that you want to remember for each one.*

CHAPTER 2
Life as Relationship

With all things and in all things,
we are relatives. —Sioux Proverb

Some have said that life is a game, and we are players. Others have called it a war, which would make us soldiers. Still others say life is a performance and we're actors on a stage playing roles. All of these ways of thinking about life are true, but they're small truths. The bigger truth is that life is a relationship.

Everywhere we look, life is in relationship on numerous levels. Socially, we each started out as a relationship between a man and a woman. On the biological level, we started out when when a sperm met an egg and these two entities began a relationship. This initial coming together in every life tells us something about the nature of all relationship. The sperm and the egg, upon meeting, immediately begin to *transform* one another until, in the end, they both together become something entirely new. Namely, you and me and all the rest of us.

This is what relationship is about: things coming together in ways that transform them. Relationship is *the* medium for transformation, the place where it happens. Nothing has ever changed that did not come into relationship with something else. Since life is change, this means there is no life without relationship. Life *is* relationship.

Consider this for a moment: Your very existence depends on continual relationship. If you could somehow get out of all relationships in your life you would, in that moment, cease to exist.

"What if I move out into the wilderness and never speak to people again?" No matter. You're still in relationship with them because they exist and have an effect on you. You share the earth. "What if I'm hit on the head and completely forget that humanity exists?" It makes no difference. You're connected on the physical level by the genes in your body, by the way your brain works, and everything else you share with people — whether you know about it or not.

The only way to get out of relationship is to get out of the whole business of existence. To exist is to be in relationship. This makes sense when we think about relationship in a slightly broader context than we're perhaps used to. For our purposes, "relationship" is any interaction between two parts of a whole or two members of a community. In this sense everything that exists is in relationship at all times because we're all interacting parts of the whole.

THE FOUR RELATIONSHIPS

To be able to think about this big relationship more easily we can break it down into four areas, four basic relationships in which we are all involved:

- ❖ Relationship with self
- ❖ Relationship with others
- ❖ Relationship with the transcendent
- ❖ Relationship with nature

We're in relationship with ourselves by virtue of the fact that, as someone wisely said, "Wherever you go, there you are."

We've already talked about our relationship with others and it seems that wherever we go, there *they* are as well.

The transcendent is that part of reality that might be called its larger aspect. Some might call it the spiritual and/or God; others may simply think of it as larger reality or the sacred. Whatever we call it, we are in relationship with it as surely as we are in relationship with

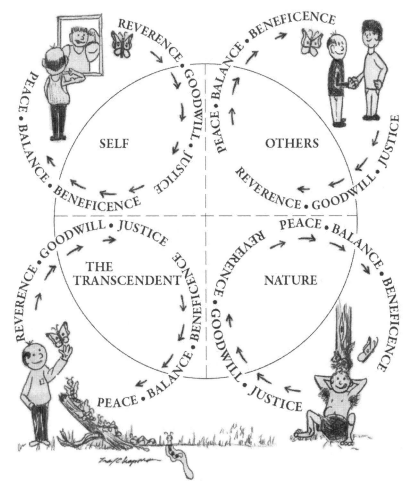

The Four Relationships

smaller reality. Wherever we go, there is the transcendent also.

Likewise, with nature: we are in relationship with it simply by virtue of being in a physical body and doing any bodily things such as eating, drinking, moving our muscles or breathing.

Point being, when it comes to relationship, we don't get to opt in or out. Even when we die our body continues to be in relationship with the earth (as worm food or ashes or simply atoms). The only choice we get in regard to relationship is whether we will be in right relationship or wrong relationship.

Right relationship is relationship that strives for and/or leads to wholeness. Wrong relationship is relationship that decreases wholeness. Remember we defined wholeness as "peace, balance and beneficence." So we can ask of any action or thought (any way of relating), "Does it increase peace, balance and beneficence?"

THE THREE ASPECTS OF RIGHT RELATIONSHIP

Three things are necessary for a relationship that increases wholeness. We call them the three aspects of right relationship:

* Reverence
* Goodwill
* Justice

Reverence is acknowledging the presence of the transcendent in people and things and inquiring into their larger meaning and purpose.

Goodwill is wanting people and things to express their transcendent meaning and purpose and move toward wholeness.

Justice is giving people and things what they need to be whole, not what we think they deserve for failing to be whole.

These three things are the foundation of all right relationship with self, others, the transcendent and nature. We're going to talk about all four of these relationships in upcoming sections, but since we use the transcendent in our definition of reverence and goodwill, I want to talk a bit more about the transcendent here.

We define the transcendent as the larger aspect of all things. So there is an "ordinary you" and a "transcendent you." That is to say, there's a part of you that goes beyond ordinary experience and existence. There's something about you that will always be a mystery, even to yourself. This is true of all reality. For this reason, the transcendent can be difficult to define. Because it is, among other things, the mysterious aspect of things. Mystery can be encountered but not explained. We can interact with it and be in relationship with it (we do it all the time), but we can't fully explain or intellectually understand it.

We've defined reverence as acknowledging the presence of the transcendent in people and things and inquiring into their larger meaning and purpose.

To acknowledge the presence of the transcendent in someone or something is to stand before the mystery of that person or thing. It is to be aware that we are looking into an ocean of depth that we can never know completely. And of course, the moment we acknowledge this, the moment we give that nod of recognition to the transcendent in others, it immediately becomes as much about us as about them. This is true because to acknowledge mystery in our world is to simultaneously be made aware of our own smallness; it is to admit that we are part of something that transcends us.

Admitting our smallness, however, paradoxically puts us in connection with our larger selves. Admitting that we are small makes us large. You know this already — that's why we think of a humble person as large-minded and an arrogant person as small-minded.

So this is reverence in a nutshell. And while reverence is certainly a good thing, it is also a scary thing, which is why we often don't practice it. It's scary for the reasons we just discussed: to practice reverence is to acknowledge our own smallness. But if we can remember that this, in turn, makes us large, we can overcome our fear.

And this is how we come to true goodwill — *wanting* people and things to express their transcendent meaning and purpose and move toward wholeness. This is something our larger self does. Our small self is incapable of goodwill because it sees any advancement made by others as a potential threat to itself. It is small-minded in this regard.

Goodwill follows and is built upon reverence. Only after acknowledging the transcendent can we then want it to be expressed.

Justice, in turn, stands on both reverence and goodwill. If we acknowledge the transcendent and want it to be expressed, then we can give people and things what they need to move closer to that. Wholistic justice is impossible to practice without first practicing reverence and goodwill.

But when we begin with reverence, goodwill becomes possible. And when we have reverence and goodwill, wholistic justice rises out of these like a plant from good soil.

The practice of these three aspects in each of the four relationships stands at the heart of wholeness ethics, so let's take a closer look at how they apply in our relationships with self, with others, with the transcendent and with nature.

IF YOU HAVE A COUPLE OF BRAIN CELLS THAT NEED SOMETHING TO DO... *Write out the four relationships in order from your strongest to your weakest relationship. If two or more are equal, put them on the same line. Was this different at different stages in your life?*

CHAPTER 3
Relationship with Self

To be yourself in a world that is constantly trying to make you something else is the greatest accomplishment. —Ralph Waldo Emerson

Talking about being in relationship with myself always makes me think of the joke about the guy who went to group therapy alone... and came out with a black eye. But we don't have to be crazy to argue with ourselves. It's very sane. In fact, it's when we stop arguing with ourselves that we're on our way to insanity.

There are times I want to go for a walk and I want to lay around at the same time. I say to myself: "I should go out and take a walk. I'm tired of lying here."

"Yeah, maybe in a minute," I respond. "For now I just want to sit here and watch TV."

"You know a walk will help keep your cholesterol down."

"Yeah, yeah," I say, annoyed as I eat another cookie.

And so it goes.

We don't usually see ourselves as being in relationship with ourselves, but we are, as surely as we are in relationship with things outside of ourselves. Examples of this include our constant inner dialogues; inner conflicts; exchanges between different parts of ourselves such as our intellect, impulses and will, and our mind and body. Each of us is, in a very real sense, a community of different parts all relating to each other. This is why it's possible to hate ourselves, be angry with ourselves, or be proud of ourselves. All these are relationships with ourselves.

How we navigate these inner differences is what determines whether we're in right or wrong relationship with ourselves. If one of these impulses is "parental" and always telling me to do what's safe, and another is "childish" and always telling me to do whatever feels good right now, there are several ways to resolve the conflict. One is to simply do what the parent in me wants — always do what's safe. If I do that I lose touch with the part of me that knows how to have fun — the child. On the other hand, I can resolve the conflict by listening only to the child in me and doing whatever makes me feel good right now. In which case I lose touch with the reasonable part of myself, the part that keeps me from destroying myself.

Neither of these solutions is very healthy and neither promotes wholeness. Trying to find some balance between these impulses is the more wholistic way to go.

The concept of balance is central to wholeness ethics. To be wholistic we have to consider and include all parts of the whole in a balanced way. In this case we're talking about our "whole self," so we have to consider and include all parts of ourselves.

Maybe anger has gotten us into trouble in the past and we think the solution to that is to shut down that angry part of ourselves, to stop listening to or including it. But there are times when anger is exactly the right thing to be feeling. If we shut it down, we throw ourselves out of balance in the opposite direction. Instead of too much anger we have too little.

The same is true of fear. It's certainly not healthy to live in constant fear, but if someone's pointing a gun at you fear may be the only thing that will help you respond quickly enough to not get shot. Fear is, in fact, the only sensible response to many situations in life.

We tend to think in terms of "negative" and "positive" feelings, but when we switch from this thinking to "wholistic" or "a-holistic" we begin to see that what's really "negative" is imbalance. Take sadness or hurt for example. There was a time in my life that I thought sadness and pain were "negative," so whenever I got hurt I would turn it into anger. If you said something that hurt my feelings I might lash out at you or try to pick a fight with you. This was an imbalance toward anger because I thought anger was more manly. Now I might still get angry but I make an effort to rebalance myself by acknowledging and allowing myself to feel the initial hurt.

This concept of balance goes beyond emotions to all aspects of our relationship with self. It applies to our dreams, our limitations, our beliefs about who we are and what we're capable of. If I have a dream of becoming an artist or a musician and tell myself that it's a waste of time to think about that because it'll never happen, I'm out of balance and not in right relationship with myself. If, on the other hand, I become obsessed with that dream and abandon my family or drive myself to destruction chasing it, I'm also out of balance and in wrong relationship.

This all connects to our three aspects of right relationship: reverence, goodwill and justice.

REVERENCE FOR SELF

Being in right relationship with ourselves is about reverence because it's about being true to who we are and what we were made for. Remember, our definition of reverence is: acknowledging the presence of the transcendent in people and things and inquiring into their larger meaning and purpose.

If we're to be in right relationship with ourselves we need first to ask "What is my larger meaning and purpose?" and then honor that in our thoughts and actions. Of course we have many things we can say we're made for — to be mothers, fathers, workers, etc. But here we're talking about our *largest* purpose, the one that's more essential, more fundamental than all others.

These are the questions central to this inquiry: "What am I?" or "Why am I here?" Is it simply to have fun? To eat and consume goods? To look better than the next guy in front of my peers?

We may never find an easy or final answer, but to be in right relationship with ourselves we must ask such questions and keep on asking

How's your relationship with your self?

them. One way to do this is to reverse it and look at what we were *not* made for. In other words, look at purposes that are too small for and not worthy of us.

We were certainly not made to be thieves or murderers. Neither was anyone made to be a victim, to be abused, cheated or harmed. On another track, were we made simply to consume, to acquire lots of goods? If not, then what might be a purpose that is worthy of us? To ask this question is the beginning of reverence — the beginning of acknowledging the presence of the transcendent in ourselves and inquiring about our larger meaning and purpose — and reverence is the beginning of right relationship.

GOODWILL FOR SELF

Next comes goodwill. If we want to be in right relationship with ourselves, we have to want to move toward the fulfillment of our larger purpose. We must *care* about whether our lives head in that direction.

How can we begin to care more about whether we fulfill our larger purpose? I was talking to a man recently who said sometimes he feels bad about being healthy and taking care of himself after hurting other people in his life. It didn't seem right for him to be doing well, finding peace, wholeness, etc.

He was having trouble having goodwill for himself. But I pointed out to him that he actually owed it to his victims to become more whole. This is true because the more whole we become the less likely we are to victimize others and vice versa — the less whole we are, the more likely it is that we'll hurt others. So which of these is more likely to benefit the world, including those we've harmed?

Having goodwill for ourselves, actually wanting ourselves to be whole and succeed, isn't selfish. It's only selfish when we think we can do it at other people's expense. When we understand that it can only be done in the larger context of right relationship, it is wholistic.

Justice for Self

Finally, we must do justice by giving ourselves what we need to move toward our larger purpose and be more whole. This, of course, can mean all sorts of different things. Sometimes what I need to give myself is a sharp rebuke, while other times I need a kind word. Sometimes I need to hold my feet to the fire, other times I need to let myself off the hook — whatever it is that moves me closer to my larger purpose is justice.

We mentioned in the previous section that these three — reverence, goodwill and justice — are built up successively. We can't have goodwill, wanting things to unfold according to their larger purpose, unless we first acknowledge the transcendent in them. Likewise, we can hardly do justice, giving things what they need, if we've never thought about what they were made for, what their larger purpose is.

Of course, if we've skipped reverence and goodwill, we don't know that we're incapable of doing justice, which is why, with no more information than we pick up in a 20-second news flash, most of us are convinced we know exactly what justice is in any given situation, even to the point that we're willing to declare exactly what punishment people deserve (usually harsh ones), and whether or not any mitigating factors should be considered (they should not). I'll never forget reading the report by a probation officer to the judge in my case prior to my sentencing. He had interviewed me once and concluded that I should be sent to prison for "a very long time" because there was "little chance" that I could ever be rehabilitated. This is the result of believing that we are capable of practicing justice without first practicing reverence or goodwill — without being in right relationship.

And before we muster too much outrage at this person's arrogance, we might want to consider another fact: I agreed with him. Maybe not about the "very long" prison term, but certainly about my chances of ever amounting to anything good. I had no more reverence for myself than he did and thus was just as incapable of deciding what justice would have been in my situation, for me or for the victims. I was only capable of thinking about what I wanted, not what I needed.

Only by later developing reverence for myself, acknowledging the presence of the transcendent in myself and inquiring into my larger meaning and purpose, did I become capable of asking about and eventually giving myself what I needed to be whole. The promise that neither I nor the probation officer could see was made visible only when I got into right relationship with myself and began practicing reverence, goodwill and justice toward myself. And, by the way, one of the things I saw more clearly was that I needed to be sent to prison. Being locked up was justice for me at that time. Seeing this is another way to participate in justice for myself — another way of giving myself what I need.

This of course changes constantly so we have to keep asking the question. When we stop asking and think we know the answer for all time, we miss the truth that what might have been just at one time becomes unjust later. Justice, like everything else, is an ongoing relationship.

So to recap, we're in relationship with ourselves because we're made up of parts interacting within a larger whole. Each one of us is a community, physically as well as psychologically. As such, we're capable of being in right or wrong relationship with ourselves. Right relationship is possible only when we keep ourselves in balance and practice reverence, goodwill and justice in our relationship with self.

One part of this balance is seeing ourselves in our larger context and this brings us to our relationship with others.

IF YOU REALLY WANT TO IMPRESS YOUR OTHER SEVEN SELVES... *Write out the transcendent mission statement for your life.*

Ask yourself the following questions:

❖ *Do I maintain an awareness of my mission as I live my daily life?*

❖ *What am I doing to realize my mission?*

❖ *How can I live a more mission-centered life?*

CHAPTER 4
Relationship with Others

The important thing in life is to be able to strike a proper balance between caring for the self and caring for the other. But Balance is not simply about arithmetic — about the number of hours we spend, or the service we give. Balance is about doing a proper amount, a necessary amount, of both. —Joan Chittister

Others. They're crazy. They're wonderful. They're mean and loving and petty and magnanimous and stupid and funny and thoughtless and thoughtful and greedy and generous. They're the cause of much of our suffering. They're where we go for much of our comfort when we suffer. They're also everywhere. Which makes some people happy and others not so much. But whether we love lots of people or prefer them in small doses we tend to put them into two categories: Those who make us happy when they show up and those who make us happy when they leave.

Right relationship with others is about including both of these groups in our moral awareness. It is, as mentioned earlier, relationship that increases wholeness in ourselves and in the world —

regardless of what others are doing. We also said that relationship is the medium for transformation and development. If you want to grow and develop you must be in relationship, and the more different kinds of relationship you engage in the more areas you will grow and develop in.

Relationships that are comfortable, with people who generally make us feel good are one kind and they're good for growth in the same way that rest is good for physical growth. But if all we do is rest then it's no longer beneficial. The same is true if we try to limit ourselves only to relationships with people who make us feel good. I say "try" because, of course, there's no avoiding difficult people even if we try. What we can change is how we think about these encounters and I'm suggesting that we see them as at least potentially positive rather than conclude too quickly that there's nothing to be gained from relationships with difficult people.

Of course, there's a difference between difficult people who may annoy or irritate us and those who are acting in ways that are outright toxic and destructive toward us. Is it possible to be in right relationship even with such people?

It is, just as it's possible to be in right relationship with someone who's physically ill. We don't despise sick people, even if what they have can harm us. Instead, we take necessary precautions to protect ourselves and continue to recognize the dignity and value of such people. This is the essence of right relationship. It doesn't mean ignoring our own well-being but rather putting this in balance with the well-being of others.

Our decision to act wholistically toward others should not depend on their behavior nor on any circumstance outside of ourselves. It is an act of (good) will and no matter how others respond to this decision, the fact that we're acting wholistically puts us in right relationship.

In other words, we treat others according to who we are (and who we want to be). If my decision to act wholistically toward you depends on your behavior, then my moral center is no longer in me, but rather outside of me. I am governed not from within, but from without.

We also treat difficult people according to who we know they are, not according to how

Whose game are you playing?

they're acting at any given moment. Imagine a good friend of yours has amnesia and has forgotten who he is. If you approach him on the street and try to help him he may ignore you or even lash out at you. He may also behave in ways that aren't normal to him. Maybe he begins saying racist things or talking about robbing a bank. He's forgotten who he is. Should we then treat him according to how he's behaving at the moment? Or is it our job to remember who he is even if he's not living up to it at the moment?

One way we restore, maintain and increase our own wholeness is by remembering who we truly are. Another way is by remembering who others are when they forget. This is wholistic because as Dr. Raymond Johnson put it: "The respect given to others rebounds to the giver; to deny the sacred in the Other is to deny it in oneself."

REVERENCE FOR OTHERS

This is a way of practicing reverence toward others — acknowledging the presence of the transcendent in them. It's a way of putting into practice the belief that people are always more than their immediate behavior or circumstances.

One way I practice this is by seeing all humanity (and all of creation for that matter) sitting in a big circle around the truth. The truth, being in the center, looks slightly different from each point on the circle.

This helps me realize that even when I think people are wrong in the way they think, I can still listen to and consider the way they see things. I don't have to adopt it, but simply acknowledge that this is their experience. I can do this because I think of us both sitting on this circle around the truth. I don't know what things look like from their point on the circle and they don't know what things look like from my point. We are each in possession of only our little wedge of truth. When we mistakenly think this little wedge is "the whole truth" we, in fact, turn it into a small truth. But when we acknowledge that our little wedge of truth is just a fraction of the whole, we give ourselves permission to listen to others, thereby gaining access to many other points on the circle. As the Danish physicist Niels Bohr said: "There are two kinds of truth, small truth and great truth. You can recognize a small truth, because its opposite is falsehood. The opposite of a great truth is another great truth."

We all have the tendency to think that the way we see things is the right way. This in turn leads to the conclusion that those who see things differently must be wrong (the small-truth/falsehood way of thinking). Seeing us all sitting on this circle around the truth allows me to see my thinking as *a* right way rather than *the* right way. It allows me to be open to other right ways of seeing.

The other day one of the guys in our group said, "Some people are just toxic, and I don't see how I can be in right relationship with them." He had a good point, but I asked him to consider this question: Can't we be in right relationship with, say, arsenic? This is certainly a toxic substance. We shouldn't treat it like sugar and put it on our breakfast cereal. But we can be in right relationship with it simply by recognizing this truth.

The same is true of toxic people. The way to be in right relationship with thieves is to not give them access to your valuables while simultaneously "acknowledging the transcendent in them and inquiring into their larger meaning and purpose."

Being in right relationship with others doesn't mean being a doormat — that would be wrong relationship with self. Wholeness ethics doesn't ask us to turn ourselves into doormats, but it does ask us to have reverence for people who sometimes don't have reverence for us — even while refusing to allow them to abuse us.

GOODWILL FOR OTHERS

After acknowledging the transcendent in people comes goodwill, wanting people to express their larger meaning and purpose. This is pretty simple. After we see the transcendent in a person, we can desire to see it unfold in that person. The "will" part of goodwill is that we have to choose to have this desire rather than its opposite — especially for a-holistic people who often do not have goodwill for us. So wanting them to express their larger meaning and purpose is often not a product of emotions or feelings, but of will. We will it because we know that no matter how others think or behave, we can only be in right relationship by practicing these three aspects – reverence, goodwill, and our next step, justice.

JUSTICE FOR OTHERS

Remember we defined justice as giving people and things what they need to be whole, not what we think they deserve for failing to be whole. So, in a sense, justice is reverence and goodwill in action.

This wholistic justice is a different animal than the retributive justice we're used to. Retributive justice, as the name implies, is about retribution. It focuses on causing people to suffer when they've caused others to suffer. It's about giving people what we think they deserve. This view of justice is very narrow. It applies, for instance, only to people, and so excludes the rest of creation from considerations of justice. What does a horse "deserve" for throwing a rider and killing her? Or what do animals "deserve" in general? It's impossible to say what they deserve, good or bad, but they do need things, thus they are included in wholistic justice but not in retributive justice. Beyond this, retributive justice excludes even the vast majority of human relations from considerations of justice because it comes into play only when a wrong of some sort has been committed. It doesn't consider justice to be in play in ordinary relations.

Wholistic justice is about increasing wholeness. It isn't just a response to wrongdoing but is something that we're called to practice at all times. It's a response to life — an ongoing principle of right relationship to be practiced in all the daily details of our lives.

When we practice this kind of justice in combination with reverence and goodwill we can be in right relationship with others no matter whether they are also practicing right relationship with us.

This view was stated by Dr. Viktor Frankl,

a survivor of Nazi concentration camps, who lost his family and almost his own life to the hideous and a-holistic thinking of Hitler and his followers. Frankl said when all else is taken away, there remains what he called "man's last freedom," which is the freedom to *choose how we will respond.* He refused, through everything he endured, to be drawn by his captors into a-holistic thinking. In other words, he would not let their behavior determine his ethical principles. Instead he kept that right for himself alone.

So too can we, no matter what others may do or how they may choose to live.

IF YOU DON'T ALREADY HAVE ENOUGH TO THINK ABOUT... *List three ways you can acknowledge the transcendent in others and three ways you have failed to do so in the past.*

CHAPTER 5
Relationship
with the Transcendent

But still, existence for us is a miracle; in a hundred places it is still the source. A playing of absolute forces that no one can touch who has not bowed down in wonder.

—*Rainer Maria Rilke*

Of the four basic relationships, this is the one that most often causes people to say "Huh?" We're all familiar with self, others, and nature, but what on earth is the transcendent and how are we in relationship with it?

We said earlier that the transcendent is the larger aspect of reality. This, of course, doesn't mean *physically* larger, but larger in nonphysical terms the way someone can "be the larger man" in a situation or the way certain ideas and attitudes can be large (minded) and small (minded).

Take, for example, a person whose whole life is centered around being a "tough guy." Such a person, depending on how obsessed he is with maintaining his tough-guy status, may never read a book on philosophy, appreciate the beauty of great art, or think an original thought. This is a small (minded) way to live.

Or take someone whose entire identity is centered around how life is mistreating them. We've all met people who are perpetually angry and always ready to tell you the latest injustice they've encountered.

Manipulators are another example. They spend their days and their mental energies trying to think up ways to manipulate others. Whether they do it for monetary gain or for the thrill of "getting over on people" so they can feel superior, it's a small way of being.

Add in people who spend their lives engaging in and/or manufacturing false dramas. Here in prison this is widespread. Grown men with families and responsibilities awaiting them beyond these fences are stabbing others for bumping them or speaking a careless word. This is nothing but a bloody version of third-grade playground antics; it's not worthy of us.

Spending our intellectual and emotional energies on such things is like a man in a vast dark gallery containing all the world's great art, scientific discoveries and intellectual thought. This man controls the only light source — his own consciousness, which lights up whatever he looks at the way a flashlight lights up objects in a dark room. He can direct it anywhere he wants. Yet he chooses to shine it on a pile of pigeon droppings at his feet and spend his entire time in the gallery complaining about the cleaning staff.

So this is what we mean by non-physical smallness. What then, does largeness look like? What is worthy of us?

Well, the examples are endless. If our tough guy expands his vision, sees more possibility and begins caring about things more important than being a tough guy, we could say that he is living a larger life. When someone steps in to smooth a situation that would have otherwise ended in violence, this is a glimpse of the transcendent in action. Or someone rescuing abused animals, standing up for the weak or showing a kindness are all moments of transcendence.

I have a friend who brings crime victims and criminal offenders together and helps them talk, which often results in healing and reconciliation. My friend's action, the forgiveness offered by the victims and the courage of the criminal to face his own culpability are expressions of the transcendent.

Is the transcendent, then, just another word for "good deeds"? No. Good deeds are *expressions* of the transcendent, not the transcendent itself. The transcendent is the substance behind such deeds. It is the substance of goodness itself.

Other expressions of the transcendent are great works of art, great sacrifices, the beauty of nature, mathematical order in the universe, the ability of consciousness to think about itself, and the wonder of a giant oak tree existing inside an acorn.

Sometimes people ask, "Is the transcendent just another name for God?" The answer is no. Wholeness ethics is neither a religion nor a religious program. Which is another way of saying wholeness ethics does not advocate or require any belief in the supernatural whatsoever.

With this said, it must be added that the reverse is also true. We don't discourage belief in God and we're in no way in competition with or hostile to religious belief. And, it's true that some people think of the transcendent as God or as an expression of God. It's also true that other people who aren't religious think of the transcendent in different terms — perhaps as goodness, beauty, truth, or even as the "great mystery." These different conceptions of the transcendent are perfectly all right and in line with the tenets of wholeness ethics.

As Ralph Waldo Emerson said, "The foregoing generations beheld God and nature face to face; we, through their eyes. Why should not we also enjoy an original relation to the universe?"

A-tree-ism

Is there really a Tree?

No. That's just a myth.

This is what wholeness ethics holds to be true about the transcendent — that it must and should be experienced personally. The more precisely someone else defines it for us, the less personal our relationship with it will be.

Imagine you are at a party and I introduce you to a woman. After introducing you, I remain standing between you. Every time you ask a question or try to look around me at her I lean over and answer your question with my observations about her. This is what it's like to give someone too specific a definition or description of the transcendent.

If you feel this section has not provided a very full definition of the transcendent, this is why. The approach of wholeness ethics is to point in the direction of the transcendent then stand out of the way. We can all talk about our individual experiences later, but we encourage an "original relation" rather than one filtered through us or anyone else.

This begins with the three aspects of right relationship — reverence, goodwill and justice.

REVERENCE FOR THE TRANSCENDENT
What is reverence toward the transcendent?

Remember, we defined reverence as acknowledging the transcendent in people and things and inquiring into their larger meaning and purpose. The beginning of reverence toward the transcendent is simply acknowledging its presence. We do this by directing the flashlight of our consciousness up away from the pigeon droppings of life and onto larger things, which we are calling the transcendent.

To practice reverence for the transcendent, I may literally look up at the night sky and acknowledge the vastness of which we are a part. Or, I may look up metaphorically by thinking big thoughts about small things such as seeds and atoms (or, pigeon droppings, for that matter).

Goodwill for the Transcendent

Goodwill is wanting people and things to express their transcendent purpose and move toward wholeness. Goodwill toward the transcendent is simply wanting it to be expressed in people and things. I've noticed that most of my thoughts can either be blessings or curses. To practice goodwill for the transcendent, I may do something as simple as bless rather than curse the world as I encounter it moment by moment.

JUSTICE FOR THE TRANSCENDENT

Lastly, justice is giving the transcendent what it may need to express itself in the people and things we encounter in our lives. This is directed, as is the goodwill and reverence, not only at the people and things in question, but at the transcendent itself. What does the transcendent need? Maybe it needs me to be its human voice, to point it out to a person or in a situation where it gets lost. There are truly an infinite number of answers to this question, so justice is better served by simply remembering and asking the question than by trying to remember all the answers. What does the transcendent need from you in this moment?

IF YOU WANT TO START LISTENING TO THE GOOD VOICES... *List three expressions of the transcendent in each of the four relationships.*

CHAPTER 6
Relationship with Nature

*Every natural fact is a symbol of
some spiritual fact. —Ralph Waldo Emerson*

Our relationship with nature has changed more in the past 100 years than it had in the 1,000 years prior. Mostly this change has been in the direction of becoming estranged from nature. Partly this happened accidentally. We didn't consider how small advances in technology and society would, when taken together, add up to big changes in our relationship with nature. But another part of it wasn't accidental at all.

Humankind has long had a love/hate relationship with nature and there is a line of thinking, especially in Western culture, that sees the physical world as "low," "vulgar," "unspiritual" and so on. This has negatively colored our thinking about sex, the environment, food, aging, death, illness and virtually every aspect of being physical.

Today, things like illness, aging, and death, which in other times might have been seen as natural cycles, are often seen as injustices. Since these things are part of the very process of life, this thinking leads to seeing that process itself as an enemy. Sex, which again, is a natural and normal part of life, is seen as "naughty" by almost all of us and as a necessary evil by the most puritan among us. As a result, much of our sexuality is either repressed or expressed pornographically.

Thinking wholistically, we can ask how intimately our strained relationship with nature is connected to things such as high rates of sexual deviance, drug addiction, obesity and eating disorders, teenage pregnancy, broken male-female relationships and violence against women.

Once we acknowledge this connection, the wholistic response to these many problems becomes clear: begin healing our relationship with nature. This, more than laws, jails, or technological, biological or pharmaceutical fixes is the response that truly addresses the problem rather than its symptoms.

What then does a healthy and wholistic relationship with nature look like? What does it mean to have reverence, goodwill and justice toward nature and toward our own naturalness?

How is your relationship with nature?

REVERENCE FOR NATURE

Reverence is acknowledging the transcendent in all things, so the first thing we're called to do is get rid of the thinking that pits the transcendent and the natural against one another. To be "spiritual" or "enlightened" isn't to be "un-physical," despite the long tradition of waging war against our bodies and the natural world to get closer to the transcendent. On the contrary, the transcendent is *in* the physical, not the *opposite* of the physical. The transcendent is *here* in every atom of creation, not "out there" in some other place.

This is why wholeness ethics refers to the transcendent and the physical as "larger and smaller" rather than using the more dualistic "higher/lower," "sacred/profane" or "true/false" language. This language of wholism allows us to see that the "small" (the purely physical) exists within the "larger" (the transcendent) but also vice versa: the transcendent exists within the physical. We become "larger" not by waging war against the physical (or even the ego) but simply by relating to these things in their larger contexts. The ego is as "spiritual" as the spirit — just as eating a hamburger can be as sacred as going to church. It's only when we fail to recognize this larger aspect of things that we strip them of context and make them "unspiritual." Seeing things wholistically is seeing both their smallness and their largeness at the same time. It's knowing that the line between large and small doesn't run between things on earth, but rather through their centers.

Science has helped me do this, by revealing more of nature to me. Everything from learning about the unfathomable distances of outer space to the magical discoveries in the other direction — the invisible subatomic realm being explored by quantum physics — has contributed to raising my esteem of the large and the small in the physical world.

Through fundamental revelations, like the truth that what we think of as "the solid world" isn't solid at all but is flowing like a river, science has shown me what might be called the "atomic intelligence" of matter, and has helped me understand that even in something as mundane as a rock, atoms are communicating with one another, bonding together in relationship to create a little community that we refer to as "rock."

The more estranged I became from nature in my adulthood the more I began to think of it as "dead," as nothing but "stuff." But what I knew as a child, that the world is alive and buzzing with possibility, I re-learned from science as an adult.

So this is one way we can practice reverence toward nature, by learning about it. But science isn't the only way to do this. We can do it by simple observation, by taking time to look for points of connection with nature, which can occur by observing our own bodies, thinking about and being more mindful of our food, or observing plants and insects and small animals around us. And asking questions is the beginning of caring, which moves us into goodwill.

GOODWILL FOR NATURE

Goodwill, you know by now, is the desire to see people and things express their larger purpose and meaning and the desire to see the transcendent unfold in them. In wholeness ethics, we don't call this "love" because the word is laden with romantic connotations in our culture, but goodwill in this sense is a non-romantic form of love. Having "a love of nature" isn't just to love using it and being entertained by it. It's wanting it to express its larger purpose and meaning.

What is this purpose and meaning? There's been an attitude in modern times that the entire purpose and meaning of nature is centered around us. Many believe, consciously or unconsciously, that nature's purpose is to serve as a combination supermarket, building-supply store and entertainment mall for human beings. This is akin to (and comes from the same worldview as) the notion that one race of humans exists to serve another. Of course nature provides us food, beauty, building supplies and energy for everything we do and have ever done, and there's nothing wrong with that, but this is not its larger purpose.

Perhaps nature's larger purpose is to know itself. If so, we could say it created human beings to serve this purpose — so it could know itself through us. This would make us nature's servant rather than the other way around. This may or may not be the case, but it's as reasonable an explanation as our current human-centered paradigms. The point is to ask the questions, not simply assume that nature is "beneath us" and therefore that it ought to be used in whatever way we see fit. If we applied this attitude to any other relationship, we would see immediately that it can only lead to wrong relationship.

JUSTICE FOR NATURE

Right relationship comes from seeing that nature, like all things, is seeking its own wholeness in its own way. When we see ourselves as being in relationship with this process in nature and begin to act in ways that give nature what it needs to move toward the fulfillment of its larger purpose, this brings justice into the space between us.

There are many areas in our time where our actions toward nature are simply unjust. This includes our treatment of the animals we raise for food and those in the wild and the way we treat the environment in general. It involves the way we think about and treat our own bodies and the ways we relate to the natural cycles of life. Said differently, we're acting in ways that do not assist nature in expressing its larger purpose and meaning, neither in human, nor in other, forms.

Modern culture has blessed us in many ways (and the wholistic view embraces these blessings) but it has also left us disconnected from one another, from ourselves, and from the earth. Disconnection leads to dysfunction. Coming back into right relationship with nature is a step toward wholeness and healing in every area of our lives.

IF YOU'RE FEELING FROGGY... *List three ways you can be in better relationship with nature.*

CHAPTER 7
Putting It All Back Together

A human being is part of the whole called by
us "universe," a part limited in time and space.
He experiences himself, his thoughts, and feelings,
as something separated from the rest — a kind of
optical delusion of his consciousness. This delusion is
a kind of prison for us, restricting us to our personal
desires and to affection for a few persons near to us.
Our task must be to free ourselves from this prison
by widening our circle of compassion to embrace all
living creatures and the whole of nature
in its beauty. —Albert Einstein

We've been talking about the four basic
relationships — with self, nature, the transcendent
and others — as separate things. Taking things
apart is a good way to gain knowledge about
them. But it's no good for gaining wisdom and
understanding. These are only gained by putting
things back together, by seeing them *wholistically*.
This is true also of the four relationships. They're
not four separate things, but four parts of one
thing. Think of it as the circle of life with the
four relationships inside it. Each relationship is
part of the circle and everything that happens in
one area affects the other areas.

Putting it all back together

We can't be in right relationship in one area while ignoring or acting a-holistically in another. Said differently, we can't respect ourselves while disrespecting others. We can't love others while having no love of nature or self. We can't truly get ahead by pushing others down.

The myth of non-connection

THE MYTH OF NON-CONNECTION

The four relationships are like organs in our bodies. Imagine if one day your brain receives this message from the liver: "Blood supply very low. Get message to heart to send more immediately."

Now imagine that your brain, instead of sending the message on to the heart, thinks to itself, "I'm sick of liver's demands. Everybody knows that

81

I'm the important one. Who does he think he is? I can do more thinking if I take an extra supply of blood and shortchange the liver."

Eventually, the liver shuts down. What then happens to the brain? Did it really get ahead (if you'll pardon the pun)?

Of course not, because everything is interconnected within our bodies. When the relationship becomes a-holistic between any two parts (when it ceases to be good for the whole), we call this disease. The same is true within the circle of life even though it's happening on such a large scale that it isn't always easy to see. Whenever I begin to act in

There are better ways to get ahead.

ways that are destructive of the whole I create disease in the larger body of which I am a part. This, of course, eventually comes back around to negatively affect me.

Really understanding this profound interconnection is the basis of all ethics. We see it in our own bodies but we also see it in families where, if one person begins to act selfishly with no regard for the whole (addiction is a good example of this) the whole family is affected. This is true even if they throw the person out; his or her absence is now an ingredient in the family dynamic. We can also see it on the larger scale of neighborhoods and communities. If one family begins to act with disregard toward the whole, the entire neighborhood is affected. Wholism is simply saying that this interconnection never stops. It runs through all reality.

To believe otherwise is to be deceived by the myth of non-connection, which leads to several other wrong and a-holistic ideas such as:

* I can harm others without harming myself;
* I can *help* others without helping myself;
* I am only affected by things close to me, not by things far away

The Circle of Moral Inclusion

One effect of this myth is the idea that certain things aren't important and have no bearing on our lives. But there's another effect of the myth of non-connection. That is that we think our own actions don't matter. We think "I'm just one person; I can't really make a difference in the world so there's no point in trying or thinking about it." From here we begin to turn down our compassion, harden our hearts, and adjust ourselves to "the way things are." The myth of non-connection, while seeming to excuse us from moral responsibility on one hand, belittles and disempowers us on the other.

To remedy the effects of the myth of non-connection, we must expand our circle of moral inclusion. The circle of moral inclusion is a circle we draw around ourselves to indicate how far our compassion and consideration will extend. It's pretty simple — those who are inside my circle get my compassion and consideration; those who are outside of it don't.

In its smallest manifestation, the circle of moral inclusion has only one person in it: me. This is complete self-centeredness. A psychologist might call it sociopathy. People who have this small a circle of moral inclusion will only ask one question when acting in the world: how does it affect me? The only time it's healthy to have this self-centered a circle of moral inclusion is when you're an infant (or, temporarily, when an animal is chewing off one of your limbs). Other than that, our circle of moral inclusion should always be bigger than our ego.

But how much bigger? Most people expand their circle to at least include immediate family. This is the first level of our evolution. Some stop there but most will evolve a bit larger still. The next expansion might be to include one's neighborhood. So now "me," "my family," and "my neighborhood" are considered before acting. This is where personal moral evolution begins to falter in our culture.

Some will expand their circle to include their race, others to include their religion or culture; still others will include their nation (usually this means an idealized image of their race, religion, culture or nation and not the actual people or reality of these groups, but that's a different point). This is where most of us draw the line. This is where we say, "My circle of moral inclusion ends here."

Wholists believe this is equivalent to drawing a circle around our emotional or mental growth and saying, "I'm done growing emotionally," or "I'm done growing mentally." But to say, "I'm done growing," is to say, "I'm done being human."

So who should be in our circle of moral inclusion? Should we expand it to include all humanity? Wholists say yes. But even this isn't enough. If we want to be wholistic about it, we must expand our circle of moral inclusion to encompass all reality. All things and beings must be given moral consideration and treated with reverence, goodwill and justice.

This belief is a sound rejection of the myth of non-connection. All things are interconnected

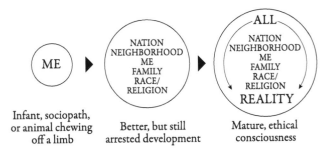

The Circle of Moral Inclusion

because all things are part of the whole. To believe otherwise is not only to abandon moral truth, it is to take leave of reality itself. Wholism, which holds that, for all our incompleteness, we still belong to each other and to the whole, is the ultimate realism.

Of course, this is the big truth, and it sounds wonderful — all things are connected, we're all brothers and sisters, etc. But who's going to tell this to the guy who steals your radio or decides he's going to be the cell-boss or treat you in any of the billion unjust and cruel ways we treat each other?

To claim that we are all part of one whole doesn't in any way deny the basic reality that most of the world isn't conscious of this and isn't, at this point, living wholistically. It simply says that the way we are right now is a small truth that sits inside the larger truth of who we are. We spoke in an earlier section about a friend having amnesia and forgetting who he or she is. Well, the same thing can happen to societies, nations and generations. Wholists are people who are trying to remember who we are, not only personally, but for us as a whole.

Thus, we live in two worlds, the world of

incompleteness and the world of (unfolding) wholeness. They're the same world. We understand that we need to deal realistically with the local and the immediate. But the moment we begin to think this is all there is and lose sight of the large and long-term, we fall out of wholism. We must strive for balance between acknowledgment of the large whole and acknowledgment of the small parts. Wholism is neither all about the large nor all about the small. Like reality itself, wholism is about both.

IF ONE SIDE OF YOUR BRAIN IS STILL TALKING TO THE OTHER... *List three ways the myth of non-connection has played out in your life.*

CHAPTER 8
The Sacred Commitment

Nothing splendid has ever been achieved except by those who dared believe that something inside them was superior to circumstance. —Bruce Barton

Many years ago I made what I've come to think of as the sacred commitment. It was after years of wrong relationship, after killing another human being, destroying my own life and devastating both our families. I was a complete failure as a human being, and when I realized this I had to make a decision.

I had several choices. First, I could try to live in denial of this reality. They say in prison you can be anything you want to be. I've seen guys who couldn't afford a tube of toothpaste pretending they owned Cadillacs and mansions and were great successes. They were living in denial of the basic reality of their lives and I could do that too if I chose to. Another option was to embrace my failure and wear it like a badge of honor. I've seen men do this as well. They play the bad-ass, brag about their crime and other exploits and are generally proud of being here (or at least pretend to be). This backwardness is a strong current in prison culture. I didn't want to contribute to it. I wasn't proud of what I'd done and didn't want to pretend otherwise.

Which brings me to my third option: Face the reality that I was a complete failure, allow myself to feel the appropriate shame for the dishonorable choices I'd made, and try to live in a more healthy and honorable way from this day forward. This was certainly the least comfortable choice but it's the one I made. This is what I'm calling the sacred commitment.

I didn't know what this way of living was nor how I was going to do it, but that didn't matter. What mattered is that I pointed myself in that direction and started walking. I didn't say, "I'll try it for awhile to see how I like it." Or, "I'll do it if it's not too hard." Instead, I said, "Come what may, good, bad, easy or difficult, this is how I will live from now on. Returning to the old way is not an option."

One of the most fundamental mistakes I've seen prisoners make over my years here is failing to take crime off the table as an option in their lives. We make all kinds of plans for the good things we're going to do when released — get our families back together, work with kids, get a job where we re-earn our reputation and regain our respect in the community, and so on. And it's all sincere. But in the back of our minds we think, "If I have to, I can deal a little dope, steal some money, etc." We keep open whatever criminal activity we know how to do so we have something to "fall back on."

The key words in this thinking are "fall" and "back." As in, fall down and end up back in prison. Even if you never get caught — and of course prisons are full of people who were never going to get caught — you're still falling down on yourself and backing away from your own self-respect.

The sacred commitment to wholeness is not saying, "I know how to do all this and how it will turn out." It's about admitting (to paraphrase Mother Teresa):

* I don't know how I'll manage to "do only what increases wholeness in myself and in the world," *but I'll do it anyway*.
* I don't know whether it will cost me friends, gain me others, or both, *but I'll do it anyway*.
* I don't know if it will be difficult or easy, *but I'll do it anyway*.
* I don't know if the parole board or anyone else will ever notice that I've changed, *but I'll do it anyway*.
* I don't know if I'll ever see all the fruits of living for wholeness, *but I'll do it anyway*.

Will you be strong enough? As John Beecher said, "Strength is a matter of a made-up mind."

For me, this was about living in ways that were worthy of me, of the life I've been given and of the many people who've come before me and sacrificed for me in ways that I will never know. It was about stepping up as a man and

Hey, nobody's perfect.
But stick together and
take care of each other.
Trust me.

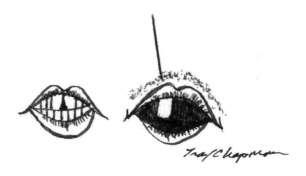

deciding to serve my larger self rather than my smaller self. It was a decision to no longer be governed by my feelings, my pain, my failures, limitations or circumstances, but rather to be governed by a clear vision based on what I love rather than what I fear. And it was about making some atonement for the harm I had caused in this world.

So I made the sacred commitment. I've stumbled and bumbled my way down this road like a blind man. I've bumped into trees, tripped over rocks, fallen in the ditch and wandered into the weeds countless times, but I'm still on the road, I'm still living my commitment. And every day I get better at it.

THE ONGOING CONVERSATION

One thing that has helped me immeasurably is something we call the "ongoing conversation." This is a "conversation" I maintain with myself, nature, others and the transcendent. I put it in quotation marks because it's not always a talking conversation. Sometimes it's silent, sometimes it's questioning, sometimes it's just saying I'm not sure how to stay wholistic in this situation. But it means always keeping wholism in my consciousness, always thinking about it, questioning some aspect of it, exploring it, digging deeper into it. It's asking how it applies to my work, how it applies to my relationship with my wife, my family, how it applies to sadness, my success, my boredom, even. Most of all, it's never thinking I've "got it" and so don't have to think about it anymore.

The ongoing conversation is a constant relationship, in one form or another, with the work of being whole and wholistic. We call it living a question-based life because answers tend to shut down conversation. "That's the way it is and there's nothing more to talk about."

When it comes to living wholistically, there's always something more to talk about. It's a lifelong journey and the ongoing conversation recognizes this. Another aspect of it is the belief that to keep anything alive we must give it away and pass it on. We, as a culture, are in the shape we're in because we have failed to pass on the truth that we should strive for wholeness and seek the practical methods of living wholistically.

The good news about this is that wholism is wholistic: part of maintaining our own commitment to it is being stewards of it in our world and in our culture. Whenever we pass it on, we strengthen our own understanding of and commitment to it. This is the ongoing conversation.

I would like to leave you with an image. Imagine that everything you've learned and everything we've discussed in this book or in the classroom version of wholeness ethics is wax that you've been putting into a jar. All this wax, pressed down and warmed up week after week, has turned into a beautiful candle.

But it's not burning. The sacred commitment is the decision to light this candle. The ongoing conversation is continuously adding wax and keeping it burning. This is work only you can do. No one else can light your candle or keep it burning, though once you do, many can help you and many will. Also, once you do, no one can put it out but you. As St. Francis of Assisi wrote, "All the darkness in the world cannot extinguish the light of a single candle."

The world and you both need the light of your candle and need you to commit to keeping it lit even when it seems your candle is the only one burning. This is the sacred commitment.

As you consider it, remember Horace Mann's admonition that, "A different world cannot be built by indifferent people."

IF YOU AGREE WITH FREDERICK DOUGLASS THAT "IT'S BETTER TO BE PART OF A GREAT WHOLE THAN THE WHOLE OF A SMALL PART"... *Face the question: "Do you commit yourself to doing only what increases wholeness in yourself and in the world?"*

Afterword

As noted in the introduction to this book, I am serving time for taking a man's life. Prior to my trial, I asked my court-appointed attorney if there was any way to communicate with the man's family. He told me I should not even attempt to make eye contact with them in the courtroom, let alone communicate in any way — it would be seen as trying to curry favor. I followed his advice, and some viewed this as a lack of remorse for what I'd done.

When I began writing this manuscript I faced a similar dilemma. And I made a decision not to discuss my crime extensively in these pages. This fact may be read by some in the same way as my silence at trial — as evidence that I do not feel remorse.

On the other hand, had I chosen to discuss my crime and my response to what I'd done more extensively, others might have seen this as evidence that I am using my crime for personal gain and that my so-called "remorse" is manufactured.

Many of my fellow prisoners will have experienced a similar Catch-22. We each have to decide how to express our remorse, but I want to encourage you to be patient with those in the larger community who may not believe you or who might demand extraordinary proof from you. Remember that they are people we've harmed and that the first casualty of every crime is basic human trust.

The bottom line is that the burden of proof ultimately falls on us, but sometimes all we can do is stop talking and keep walking the path toward wholeness.

In my case, looking squarely at my crime, owning it and feeling grief for the people I've harmed is something that I do every day, in some way, and will do until the day I die. Indeed, this book, and the whole philosophy of wholeness ethics is an expression of this. But I believe a detailed discussion of this in this venue could potentially hurt or offend some people.

I will certainly discuss any aspect of my crime at any length with the victim's family if ever they indicate a desire to do so. But to do so publicly, without knowing whether this is something they would want me to do would, in my mind, be disrespectful to them.

Someone will disagree with whatever choice I make in this matter so I have tried to handle it in the way I think is most respectful of the victim's memory and his family.

Appendixes

Wholeness Ethics and the Convict's Code

The convict's code is a blueprint for being a prisoner — not just being in prison but thinking of and identifying ourselves as prisoners. Thus when we adopt this code we're literally joining forces with the prison, despite the delusion that we're undermining and acting contrary to it. If prison is a square hole, the norms and values of the convict's code are designed to square you up so you fit perfectly here.

As such, it's more rightly called the "prison's code" than the "convict's code." Adopting it is like getting kidnapped by the circus and adopting a "clown's code."

That might make life easier in your immediate situation by making you a better fit with it, but the cost is that once you fit yourself to the circus it's that much more difficult to fit in anywhere else. When you walk down the street with your red nose, orange hair, striped pants and giant shoes, everyone who sees you immediately thinks you belong to the circus. The same is true of those who adopt the prison's code. It might ease daily life here but it renders one unfit for healthy society.

Only in a dysfunctional culture is it "honorable" to beat a guy in the head with a padlock for refusing to pay back a bar of  soap or because he bumped you on the yard, or to lie, cheat and steal. In healthy society, this is the behavior of a loser. Not just a loser, but a guy the whole world thinks needs to be locked up — a guy the world thinks is a clown who needs to be sent back to the circus.

Wholeness ethics is a true code of honor in that it is a refusal to sell ourselves out for the expedience and comfort of getting along and fitting in. It's a call to step up to bigger definitions of ourselves and a refusal to step down and allow ourselves to be defined by this or any other circus.

There are prisoners and there are men in prison. Our job is to remember the difference.

Is Wholism Logical?

Consider the wholism syllogism.

A syllogism is a form of logical argument in which two general premises lead to a specific and logical conclusion. For example:

* Premise 1: All people are mortal
* Premise 2: All Americans are people
* Conclusion: All Americans are mortal

One of the most often asked questions about wholeness ethics that we run into is: Why should I care about being wholistic? This syllogism expresses the basic logic of wholism and wholeness ethics:

* Premise 1: I am part of the whole
* Premise 2: Everything that happens within the whole affects me for good or for ill
* Conclusion: Therefore, I should care about and contribute to the health and well-being of the whole

Characteristics of Wholistic and A-Holistic Thinking

Wholistic Thinking...	**A-holistic Thinking...**
...seeks communion	...seeks to consume
...seeks to influence	...seeks to control
...thinks about us together	...thinks about me first
...is empathetic	...is apathetic
...generates peace	...generates turmoil
...generates harmony	...generates conflict
...tries to be unoffendable	...is easily offended
...sees beneath surface	...sees only surface
...seeks dialog	...seeks debate
...thinks metaphorically	...thinks literally
...is comfortable with paradox	...finds paradox unbearable
...is compassionate	...is contemptuous
...is amiable	...is contentious
...admits flaws	...hides flaws
...lives beyond circumstances	...is defined by circumstances

Glossary of Terms

A-HOLISM (A-HOLISTIC): Thinking or behavior that is not wholistic; that which decreases wholeness in oneself and in the world.

BALANCE: Right relationship between opposing, contrasting or interacting elements.

BENEFICENCE: Beneficial energy, thought or action.

CIRCLE OF MORAL INCLUSION: The amount of the world that one considers to be worthy of moral consideration; how far we believe our moral obligations extend.

DYSFUNCTIONAL: Not healthy, not sound.

ETHICS: A set of moral principles or values; the discipline dealing with what is good and bad, right and wrong.

FOUR BASIC RELATIONSHIPS: At the center of wholeness ethics, they are relationship with self, relationship with others, relationship with the transcendent, and relationship with nature.

GOODWILL: Wanting people and things to express their transcendent meaning and purpose and move toward wholeness.

INTEGRITY: Wholeness, soundness; moral health.

JUSTICE: Giving people and things what they need to be whole, not what we think they deserve for failing to be whole.

MYTH OF NON-CONNECTION: The erroneous belief that some things and people on earth are not connected to one another.

ONGOING CONVERSATION: An ongoing dialog in our own thinking, in our communities, and in our lives about, and in the pursuit of, wholeness. A never-ending inquiry into wholeness.

PEACE: The energy of well-being and enoughness.

RELATIONSHIP: Any interaction between two or more members of a community or two or more parts of a larger whole.

REVERENCE: Acknowledging the presence of the transcendent in people and things and inquiring into their larger meaning and purpose.

RIGHT RELATIONSHIP: Relationship that increases wholeness in yourself and in the world. Relationship built upon reverence, goodwill, and justice. (See *Three aspects of right relationship.*)

SACRED COMMITMENT: The unconditional commitment to wholeness as a way of life and as a measure of success. A life commitment to advance wholeness in ourselves and in the world.

THREE ASPECTS OF RIGHT RELATIONSHIP: Three things that must be present in any relationship to make it healthy and wholistic. They are *reverence, goodwill* and *justice*.

TRANSCENDENT, THE: The larger aspect and deeper significance of reality.

WHOLENESS: Peace, balance and beneficence.

WHOLENESS ETHICS: The philosophy of doing only what increases wholeness in oneself and in the world. The set of moral principles that comprise this philosophy.

WHOLISM: Thinking and action that a) considers the whole and b) advances wholeness in oneself and in the world.

WRONG RELATIONSHIP: Relationship that decreases wholeness. (See *a-holism.*)

Acknowledgments

I would like to thank the following people for their support and contributions to this book.

* The extraordinary women in my life who have shaped my soul with their love: Maryann Gorman, Amanda Chapman (aka "Mom"), Mable Chapman, Dawn Lake-Allbee, Marguerite Feller, Cari Boroff, Daphne Kingma and Nina Norell.

* All my family, whom I love but cannot count. I have thought of you and been inspired by you endless times as I've worked on this project and on wholeness ethics in general. I love you all.

* All the good men I've known over the years in prison who have found their own way to wholeness and who do their best to pass it on: Dell K. and Tony L., I'm glad you're able to have me for a cellie. Will P., Steve R., and Donny W., thanks for putting up with my clacking typewriter. The rest of you old-heads know who you are. Keep stepping up. You make a difference whether you see it or not.

❖ The men of the Kinross Ethics Project who have shown me in numerous ways what stepping up means. Keep goin' wholistic. Also, the staff who have allowed and supported the project here. Thank you.

❖ Phil B., Adam G., Grant G., Tony P., Dave M., Tom T., Brad A., Rich K., Flivver and Derb, a special gang of scoundrels who have encouraged me, challenged me, and generally put up with me over the years until I am forced to publicly call you friends.

❖ Sharon Denomme and Michael Denomme, for your generosity, friendship and sponsorship of the Ethics Project and this work on many levels. What can I say? Deep thanks. Also, the folks at Resources for Human Development for their ongoing kindness.

❖ Lisa Daly, who is responsible for the fantastic layout and design of this book. Thanks for this work, for past donations of your skills and for believing in the cause. You're a good'un.

❖ Charlotte MacNeice, Ro Goldberg, Rick Goldberg, Hubert Genz and Marie-Laure Requillart-Genz, who have loved me, cheered me on and come from faraway lands to visit me. You guys hold me up.

❖ My father, Kenneth Chapman, and Wayne Chapman, Lee Dyer, Dan MacNeice and Ron Carlson, who didn't get to see this but who all contributed by showing me, each in their own way, what it means to be a man.

❖ And all the Friends of Troy, readers of sacredmatters.blogspot.com (and hopefully wholenessethics.org) who encouraged me to be more, as a writer and a human being, with your spoken and unspoken "amens." You keep my bubble in the middle.

Whatever's good here, you've all had a part in it.

About the Author

Since his conviction in 1985 on a charge of second degree murder, Troy Chapman has been committed to changing himself and making a difference in the world. Writing has been an integral part of this commitment. His writing has been reprinted or used nationally and internationally by editors, authors, teachers, and leaders of religious organizations as touchstones in articles, magazines, books, sermons and classroom discussions and has been heard on National Public Radio. Many of Troy's essays can be found at www.sacredmatters.blogspot.com and at the "Troy's Writings" link at www.friendsoftroychapman.blogspot.com.

Still incarcerated, Troy volunteers his time in prison facilitating the Ethics Project.

If you are a prisoner or otherwise cannot order this book from the internet, write to The Whole Way Press, PO Box 922, Royersford, PA 19468.

To read more about wholeness ethics, go to www.wholenessethics.org.

Made in the USA
Lexington, KY
29 June 2019